LAIYAH THE LADYBUG

Laiyah & Cameo Thomas

Life Chronicles Publishing

ISBN: 978-1-950649-92-1

Editor: Sharon Blake

Illustrator Christine Rudinko

Life Chronicles Publishing Copyright © 2021

lifechroniclespublishing.com

This book is dedicated to my family,
classmates, teachers and all the families in the world.

CHIRP! CHIRP! CHIRP!
Ladybug Laiyah woke up to the beautiful song of the birds. She stretched her arms and fluttered her wings, trying to banish all the sleep away.

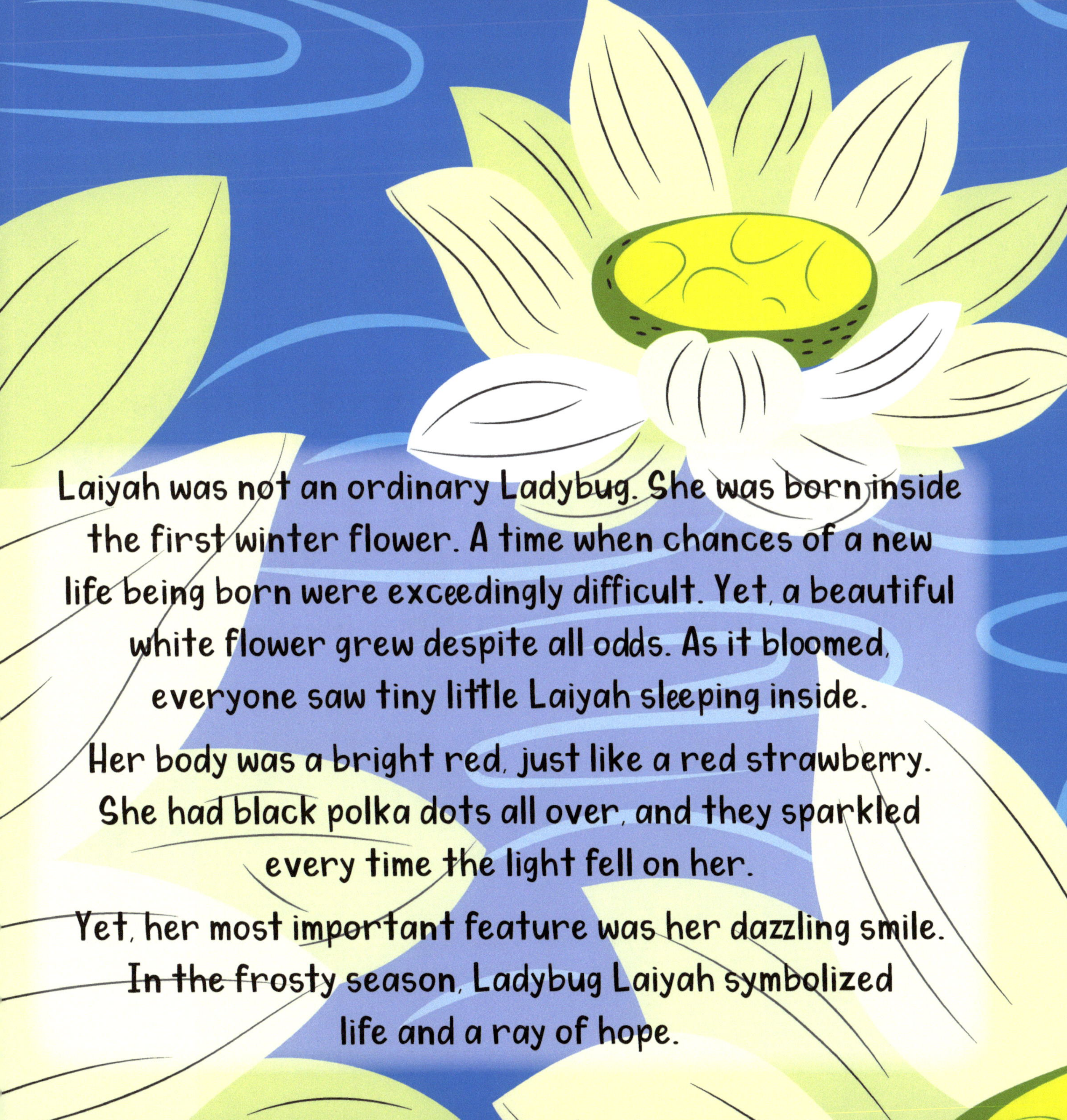

Laiyah was not an ordinary Ladybug. She was born inside the first winter flower. A time when chances of a new life being born were exceedingly difficult. Yet, a beautiful white flower grew despite all odds. As it bloomed, everyone saw tiny little Laiyah sleeping inside.

Her body was a bright red, just like a red strawberry. She had black polka dots all over, and they sparkled every time the light fell on her.

Yet, her most important feature was her dazzling smile. In the frosty season, Ladybug Laiyah symbolized life and a ray of hope.

This fine morning, Ladybug decided to take to the skies. She hadn't gone far when she saw a small crowd. A group of adults and children were sitting facing a stage.

"The local school is holding some event" Ladybug Laiyah whispered to herself. As she hovered above the ground, she saw something else.

"What's René doing there?" She questioned.

René was standing away from the entire gathering.
As Ladybug flew closer, she saw how nervous René looked.
There was sweat on her forehead, and she was biting
her nails. Laiyah knew she had to help her!

Ladybug landed on René's shoulder and gently touched
her face. "What's the matter René?" René's eyes lit up
when she saw her. "Oh, Ladybug Laiyah, you're just
the person I need."

Laiyah gave René her most hopeful smile. With Ladybug on her side, René suddenly felt a little better. She gave a small smile to Ladybug and told her everything.

It turns out today was the inter-school drama competition. It was René and her class's first performance, and the only problem was that René was too scared to face the crowd.

What if I forget my lines!
What if everyone laughs
at me! What if my class
loses because of me!!!"
René ranted.

Everything is alright!
Everything is alright!
Everything is alright!
Everything is alright!
Everything
is
is alright!
Everything
is alright!
Everything is alright!
Everything is alright!
Everything is alright!

Ladybug replied, "You need to calm down first."

"Close your eyes and imagine yourself on the stage as a bright star." Ladybug said. "And tell yourself everything is going to be okay."

René did as Ladybug said and repeated the words.

"Always remember to encourage yourself with positive words. If you think great, you'll do great!" Laiyah said.

René then opened her eyes, "Oh Ladybug thank you! I really do feel better."

Then, Ladybug Laiyah gave René a high five for extra courage. René had brighter energy around her as she joined her classmates. Ladybug knew she was going to be a famous actress one day.

Laiyah then took off and flew away.

She was flying over a basketball court when she spotted Preston, and he was holding a new basketball. Yet, he was sitting on the ground instead of playing with it.

"Why the sad face?" Ladybug asked with concern.

She gave Preston a bright smile hoping to lift his spirits. When Preston saw Laiyah, he felt a little better, and he knew there was someone he could share his problems with.

"Ladybug Laiyah, I can't score a basket no matter how hard I try." Preston began. "All my friends can. They even know how to do fancy tricks!"

Laiyah sat on Preston's hand and patted it with love.

"Preston, don't compare yourself with other people. We are all different and special in our own way. What really matters is to improve ourselves, not to get ahead of others." Ladybug told him.

"And no matter how much time it takes we never give up because failure only helps us get better," Laiyah said.

Preston finally smiled, "Well I did learn what I had been doing wrong..." Ladybug nodded, then pointed at the basketball, "You can do it!"

Preston then got up and tried to score a basket again, and he didn't score the first time or the second time, but he finally made it the third time.

After celebrating with Preston, Ladybug was back in the air. She hadn't flown far when she saw Ace.

She was confused because his owner was nowhere close.

Laiyah quickly flew over to him, "Ace, what's wrong? Where's Mayah?"

Ace, who looked on the verge of tears, seemed relieved at the sight of Ladybug. He felt that he was no longer lonely, and there was hope for him.

"Oh, Ladybug Laiyah!" Ace cried. "I'm lost! I don't know where Mayah is. We got separated."

"It's okay, Ace." Ladybug said smoothly. "I'll help you. Just stay here and I'll try to find Mayah."

Ladybug quickly flew away and tried to find Mayah.

"Aha!" Laiyah said, spotting Mayah.
She was sitting by a pond, head in
her hand. Ladybug felt her pain.

She quickly flew back to Ace and said, "I've found, Mayah! Come with me." "Oh, thank you!" Ace cried and ran after Laiyah.

Ace barked in joy when he finally caught sight of Mayah. Mayah looked up, and her face lit up with joy. The two met midway, hugging each other.

Mayah pulled back, looking at Ladybug, "Ladybug Laiyah whenever I see you, you've always helped me! Thank you so much."

Ladybug smiled, "I just want you all to be happy."

That is what Ladybug's life was all about. She wanted to help as many people as possible to find hope and happiness.

Later that day, Laiyah was having a quick snack in a flowerpot. That's when she heard a baby's cry.

She quickly looked around and saw through a window near her that a new baby girl had been born. The mom was holding the baby, with the dad hugging her.

They had tears of happiness in their eyes. Yet, there was worry in them too. Ladybug looked at the girl closely. That's when she realized the baby seemed very small. Smaller than usual. Small and fragile.

FINISH
1

Yet, the baby had a glow that only Ladybug Laiyah could see, and it called to her.

So, she flew inside, gently landed on the baby girl's forehead, kissed it, and let her magic flow.

Ladybug's powers helped her to see into the future. The baby girl saw how she would grow up to be a healthy, beautiful, and strong young lady.

As Ladybug came out of the vision, the baby smiled and opened her eyes. The parents were already looking at their little girl; for some reason, they now had hope.

"Is she going to be okay?" The Dad asked nervously.

"Your baby girl will be just fine." Ladybug Laiyah smiled. "Your love will make her a very strong young lady."

The new parents shared relieved smiles. Then they hugged and kissed their baby. Ladybug smiled at the family. She left them to enjoy this special time as a family.

The entire day had been full of adventures. She helped so many. Ladybug Laiyah was proud of how happy they all looked. To her, she could not have spent her day any better.

A life spent helping others was a life well spent.

About the Authors

Laiyah and Cameo Thomas, the mother-daughter duo, are set to shake the world of children's fiction with their work. Laiyah Thomas is a bright seven-year-old with endless energy that helps her express herself through drawing, writing, dancing, basketball, and soccer. Her heartfelt warm smile is a beacon of hope and a force of good. She is her parent's miracle, fourth child. 

Cameo Thomas is a published author and life coach.